The World of Animals

Teacher Supplement

1:1

Answers
IN GENESIS™

D1512612

GOD'S
ESIGN®

4th Edition
Debbie & Richard Lawrence

God's Design for Life
The World of Animals Teacher Supplement

Printed January 2016

Fourth edition. Copyright © 2008, 2016 by Debbie & Richard Lawrence.

ISBN: 978-1-62691-431-5

Published by Answers in Genesis, 2800 Bullittsburg Church Rd., Petersburg KY 41080

Book designer: Diane King
Editor: Gary Vaterlaus

The publisher and authors have made every reasonable effort to ensure that the activities recommended in this book are safe when performed as instructed but assume no responsibility for any damage caused or sustained while conducting the experiments and activities. It is the parents', guardians', and/or teachers' responsibility to supervise all recommended activities.

Printed in China.

AnswersInGenesis.org   •   GodsDesign.com

Welcome to GOD'S DESIGN®

LIFE

God's Design for Life is a series that has been designed for use in teaching life science to elementary and middle school students. It is divided into three books: *The World of Plants*, *The World of Animals*, and *The Human Body*. Each book has 35 lessons including a final project that ties all of the lessons together.

In addition to the lessons, special features in each book include biographical information on interesting people as well as fun facts to make the subject more fun.

Although this is a complete curriculum, the information included here is just a beginning, so please feel free to add to each lesson as you see fit. A resource guide is included in the appendices to help you find additional information and resources. A list of supplies needed is included at the beginning of each lesson, while a master list of all supplies needed for the entire series can be found in the appendices.

Answer keys for all review questions, worksheets, quizzes, and the final exam are included here. Repro-ducible student worksheets and tests may be found in the digital download that comes with the purchase of the curriculum. You may download these files from GodsDesign.com/Life.

If you prefer the files on a CD-ROM, you can order that from Answers in Genesis at an additional cost by calling 800-778-3390.

If you wish to get through all three books of the *Life* series in one year, plan on covering approximately three lessons per week. The time required for each lesson varies depending on how much additional information you include, but plan on about 40 to 45 minutes.Quizzes may be given at the conclusion of each unit and the final exam may be given after lesson 34.

If you wish to cover the material in more depth, you may add additional information and take a longer period of time to cover all the material, or you could choose to do only one or two of the books in the series as a unit study.

Why Teach Life Science?

Maybe you hate science or you just hate teaching it. Maybe you love science but don't quite know how to teach it to your children. Maybe science just doesn't seem as important as some of those other subjects you need to teach. Maybe you need a little moti-vation. If any of these descriptions fits you, then please consider the following.

It is not uncommon to question the need to teach your kids hands-on science in elementary school. We could argue that the knowledge gained in science will be needed later in life in order for your children to be more productive and well-rounded adults. We could argue that teaching your children science also teaches them logical and inductive thinking and reasoning skills, which are tools they will need to be more successful. We could argue that science is a necessity in this technological world in which we live. While all of these arguments are true, not one of them is the real reason that we should teach our children science. The most important reason to teach science in elementary school is to give your children an understanding that God is our Creator, and the Bible can be trusted. Teaching science from a creation perspective is one of the best ways to reinforce your children's faith in God and to help them counter the evolutionary propaganda they face every day.

God is the Master Creator of everything. His handiwork is all around us. Our Great Creator put in place all of the laws of physics, biology, and chemistry. These laws were put here for us to see His wisdom and power. In science, we see the hand of God at work more than in any other subject. Romans 1:20 says, "For since the creation of the world His invisible attributes are clearly seen, being understood by the things that are made, even His eternal power and Godhead, so that they [men] are without excuse." We need to help our children see God as Creator of the world around them so they will be able to recognize God and follow Him.

The study of life science helps us understand the balance of nature so that we can be good stewards of our bodies, the plants, and the animals around us. It helps us appreciate the intricacies of life and the wonders of God's creation. Understanding the world of living things from a biblical point of view will prepare our children to deal with an ecology-obsessed world. It is critical to teach our children the truth of the Bible, how to evaluate the evidence, how to distinguish fact from theory and to realize that the evidence, rightly interpreted, supports biblical creation, not evolution.

It's fun to teach life science! It's interesting, too. Children have a natural curiosity about living things, so you won't have to coax them to explore the world of living creatures. You just have to direct their curiosity and reveal to them how interesting life science can be.

Finally, teaching life science is easy. It's all around us. Everywhere we go, we are surrounded by living things. You won't have to try to find strange materials for experiments or do dangerous things to learn about life.

How Do I Teach Science?

In order to teach any subject you need to understand how people learn. People learn in different ways. Most people, and children in particular, have a dominant or preferred learning style in which they absorb and retain information more easily.

If a student's dominant style is:

Auditory He needs not only to hear the information but he needs to hear himself say it. This child needs oral presentation as well as oral drill and repetition.
Visual She needs things she can see. This child responds well to flashcards, pictures, charts, models, etc.
Kinesthetic He needs active participation. This child remembers best through games, hands-on activities, experiments, and field trips.

Also, some people are more relational while others are more analytical. The relational student needs to know why this subject is important, and how it will affect him personally. The analytical student, however, wants just the facts.

If you are trying to teach more than one student, you will probably have to deal with more than one learning style. Therefore, you need to present your lessons in several different ways so that each student can grasp and retain the information.

Grades 3–8

The first part of each lesson should be completed by all upper elementary and junior high students. This is the main part of the lesson containing a reading section, a hands-on activity that reinforces the ideas in the reading section (blue box), and a review section that provides review questions and application questions.

Grades 6–8

In addition, for middle school/junior high age students, we provide a "Challenge" section that contains more challenging material as well as additional activities and projects for older students (green box).

We have included periodic biographies to help your students appreciate the great men and women who have gone before us in the field of science.

We suggest a threefold approach to each lesson:

Introduce the topic

We give a brief description of the facts. Frequently you will want to add more information than the essentials given in this book. In addition to reading this section aloud (or having older children read it on their own), you may wish to do one or more of the following:

- Read a related book with your students.
- Write things down to help your visual learners.
- Give some history of the subject. We provide some historical sketches to help you, but you may want to add more.
- Ask questions to get your students thinking about the subject.

Make observations and do experiments

- Hands-on projects are suggested for each lesson. This part of each lesson may require help from the teacher.
- Have your students perform the activity by themselves whenever possible.

Review

- The "What did we learn?" section has review questions.
- The "Taking it further" section encourages students to
  - Draw conclusions
  - Make applications of what was learned
  - Add extended information to what was covered in the lesson
- The "FUN FACT" section adds fun or interesting information.

By teaching all three parts of the lesson, you will be presenting the material in a way that children with any learning style can both relate to and remember.

Also, this approach relates directly to the scientific method and will help your students think more scientifically. The *scientific method* is just a way to examine a subject logically and learn from it. Briefly, the steps of the scientific method are:

1. Learn about a topic.
2. Ask a question.
3. Make a hypothesis (a good guess).
4. Design an experiment to test your hypothesis.
5. Observe the experiment and collect data.
6. Draw conclusions. (Does the data support your hypothesis?)

Note: It's okay to have a "wrong hypothesis." That's how we learn. Be sure to help your students understand why they sometimes get a different result than expected.

Our lessons will help your students begin to approach problems in a logical, scientific way.

How Do I Teach Creation vs. Evolution?

We are constantly bombarded by evolutionary ideas about living things in books, movies, museums, and even commercials. These raise many questions: Did dinosaurs really live millions of years ago? Did man evolve from apes? Which came first, Adam and Eve or the cavemen? Where did living things come from in the first place? The Bible answers these questions and this book accepts the historical accuracy of the Bible as written. We believe this is the only way we can teach our children to trust that everything God says is true.

There are five common views of the origins of life and the age of the earth:

Historical biblical account	Progressive creation	Gap theory	Theistic evolution	Naturalistic evolution
Each day of creation in Genesis is a normal day of about 24 hours in length, in which God created everything that exists. The earth is only thousands of years old, as determined by the genealogies in the Bible.	The idea that God created various creatures to replace other creatures that died out over millions of years. Each of the days in Genesis represents a long period of time (day-age view) and the earth is billions of years old.	The idea that there was a long, long time between what happened in Genesis 1:1 and what happened in Genesis 1:2. During this time, the "fossil record" was supposed to have formed, and millions of years of earth history supposedly passed.	The idea that God used the process of evolution over millions of years (involving struggle and death) to bring about what we see today.	The view that there is no God and evolution of all life forms happened by purely naturalistic processes over billions of years.

Any theory that tries to combine the evolutionary time frame with creation presupposes that death entered the world before Adam sinned, which contradicts what God has said in His Word. The view that the earth (and its "fossil record") is hundreds of millions of years old damages the gospel message. God's completed creation was "very good" at the end of the sixth day (Genesis 1:31). Death entered this perfect paradise *after* Adam disobeyed God's command. It was the punishment for Adam's sin (Genesis 2:16–17; 3:19; Romans 5:12–19). Thorns appeared when God cursed the ground because of Adam's sin (Genesis 3:18).

The first animal death occurred when God killed at least one animal, shedding its blood, to make clothes for Adam and Eve (Genesis 3:21). If the earth's "fossil record" (filled with death, disease, and thorns) formed over millions of years before Adam appeared (and before he sinned), then death no longer would be the penalty for sin. Death, the "last enemy" (1 Corinthians 15:26), diseases (such as cancer), and thorns would instead be part of the original creation that God labeled "very good." No, it is clear that the "fossil record" formed some time *after* Adam sinned—not many millions of years before. Most fossils were formed as a result of the worldwide Genesis Flood.

When viewed from a biblical perspective, the scientific evidence clearly supports a recent creation by God, and not naturalistic evolution and millions of years. The volume of evidence supporting the biblical creation account is substantial and cannot be adequately covered in this book. If you would like more information on this topic, please see the resource guide in the appendices. To help get you started, just a few examples of evidence supporting biblical creation are given below:

Evolutionary Myth: Humans have been around for more than one million years.

The Truth: If people have been on earth for a million years, there would be trillions of people on the earth today, even if we allowed for worst-case plagues, natural disasters, etc. The number of people on earth today is about 6.5 billion. If the population had grown at only a 0.01% rate (today's rate is over 1%) over 1 million years, there could be 10^{43} people today (that's a number with 43 zeros after it)! Repopulating the earth after the Flood would only require a population growth rate of 0.5%, half of what it is today.

John D. Morris, *The Young Earth* (Colorado Springs: Creation Life Publishers, 1994), pp. 70–71. See also "Billions of People in Thousands of Years?" at www.answersingenesis.org/go/billions-of-people.

Evolutionary Myth: Man evolved from an ape-like creature.

The Truth: All so-called "missing links" showing human evolution from apes have been shown to be either apes, humans, or deliberate hoaxes. These links remain missing.

Duane T. Gish, *The Amazing Story of Creation from Science and the Bible* (El Cajon: Institute for Creation Research, 1990), pp. 78–83.

Evolutionary Myth: All animals evolved from lower life forms.

The Truth: While Darwin predicted that the fossil record would show numerous transitional fossils, even more than 145 years later, all we have are a handful of disputable examples. For example, there are no fossils showing something that is part way between a dinosaur and a bird. Fossils show that a snail has always been a snail; a squid has always been a squid. God created each animal to reproduce after its kind (Genesis 1:20–25).

Ibid., pp. 36, 53–60.

Evolutionary Myth: Dinosaurs evolved into birds.

The Truth: Flying birds have streamlined bodies, with the weight centralized for balance in flight; hollow bones for lightness, which are also part of their breathing system; powerful muscles for flight; and very sharp vision. And birds have two of the most brilliantly-designed structures in nature—their feathers and special lungs. It is impossible to believe that a reptile could make that many changes over time and still survive.

Gregory Parker et al., *Biology: God's Living Creation* (Pensacola: A Beka Books, 1997), pp. 474–475.

Evolutionary Myth: Thousands of changes over millions of years resulted in the creatures we see today.

The Truth: What is now known about human and animal anatomy shows the body structures, from the cells to systems, to be infinitely more complex than was believed when Darwin published his work in 1859. Many biologists and especially microbiologists are now saying that there is no way these complex structures could have developed by natural processes.

Ibid., pp. 384–385.

Since the evidence does not support their theories, evolutionists are constantly coming up with new ways to try to support what they believe. One of their ideas is called punctuated equilibrium. This theory of evolution says that rapid evolution occurred in small isolated populations, and left no evidence in the fossil record. There is no evidence for this, nor any known mechanism to cause these rapid changes. Rather, it is merely wishful thinking. We need to teach our children the difference between science and wishful thinking.

Despite the claims of many scientists, if you examine the evidence objectively, it is obvious that evolution and millions of years have not been proven. You can be confident that if you teach that what the Bible says is true, you won't go wrong. Instill in your student a confidence in the truth of the Bible in all areas. If scientific thought seems to contradict the Bible, realize that scientists often make mistakes, but God does not lie. At one time scientists believed that the earth was the center of the universe, that living things could spring from non-living things, and that blood-letting was good for the body. All of these were believed to be scientific facts but have since been disproved, but the Word of God remains true. If we use modern "science" to interpret the Bible, what will happen to our faith in God's Word when scientists change their theories yet again?

Integrating the Seven C's

The Seven C's is a framework in which all of history, and the future to come, can be placed. As we go through our daily routines we may not understand how the details of life connect with the truth that we find in the Bible. This is also the case for students. When discussing the importance of the Bible you may find yourself telling students that the Bible is relevant in everyday activities. But how do we help the younger generation see that? The Seven C's are intended to help.

The Seven C's can be used to develop a biblical worldview in students, young or old. Much more than entertaining stories and religious teachings, the Bible has real connections to our everyday life. It may be hard, at first, to see how many connections there are, but with practice, the daily relevance of God's Word will come alive. Let's look at the Seven C's of History and how each can be connected to what the students are learning.

Creation

God perfectly created the heavens, the earth, and all that is in them in six normal-length days around 6,000 years ago.

This teaching is foundational to a biblical worldview and can be put into the context of any subject. In science, the amazing design that we see in nature—whether in the veins of a leaf or the complexity of your hand—is all the handiwork of God. Virtually all of the lessons in *God's Design for Science* can be related to God's creation of the heavens and earth.

Other contexts include:

Natural laws—any discussion of a law of nature naturally leads to God's creative power.

DNA and information—the information in every living thing was created by God's supreme intelligence.

Mathematics—the laws of mathematics reflect the order of the Creator.

Biological diversity—the distinct kinds of animals that we see were created during the Creation Week, not as products of evolution.

Art—the creativity of man is demonstrated through various art forms.

History—all time scales can be compared to the biblical time scale extending back about 6,000 years.

Ecology—God has called mankind to act as stewards over His creation.

Corruption

After God completed His perfect creation, Adam disobeyed God by eating the forbidden fruit. As a result, sin and death entered the world, and the world has been in decay since that time. This point is evident throughout the world that we live in. The struggle for survival in animals, the death of loved ones, and the violence all around us are all examples of the corrupting influence of sin.

Other contexts include:

Genetics—the mutations that lead to diseases, cancer, and variation within populations are the result of corruption.

Biological relationships—predators and parasites result from corruption.

History—wars and struggles between mankind, exemplified in the account of Cain and Abel, are a result of sin.

Catastrophe

God was grieved by the wickedness of mankind and judged this wickedness with a global Flood. The Flood covered the entire surface of the earth and killed all air-breathing creatures that were not aboard the Ark. The eight people and the animals aboard the Ark replenished the earth after God delivered them from the catastrophe.

The catastrophe described in the Bible would naturally leave behind much evidence. The studies of geology and of the biological diversity of animals on the planet are two of the most obvious applications of this event. Much of scientific understanding is based on how a scientist views the events of the Genesis Flood.

Other contexts include:

Biological diversity—all of the birds, mammals, and other air-breathing animals have populated the earth from the original kinds which left the Ark.

Geology—the layers of sedimentary rock seen in road-cuts, canyons, and other geologic features are testaments to the global Flood.

Geography—features like mountains, valleys, and plains were formed as the floodwaters receded.

Physics—rainbows are a perennial sign of God's faithfulness and His pledge to never flood the entire earth again.

Fossils—Most fossils are a result of the Flood rapidly burying plants and animals.

Plate tectonics—the rapid movement of the earth's plates likely accompanied the Flood.

Global warming/Ice Age—both of these items are likely a result of the activity of the Flood. The warming we are experiencing today has been present since the peak of the Ice Age (with variations over time).

Confusion

God commanded Noah and his descendants to spread across the earth. The refusal to obey this command and the building of the tower at Babel caused God to judge this sin. The common language of the people was confused and they spread across the globe as groups with a common language. All people are truly of "one blood" as descendants of Noah and, originally, Adam.

The confusion of the languages led people to scatter across the globe. As people settled in new areas, the traits they carried with them became concentrated in those populations. Traits like dark skin were beneficial in the tropics while other traits benefited populations in northern climates, and distinct people groups, not races, developed.

Other contexts include:

Genetics—the study of human DNA has shown that there is little difference in the genetic makeup of the so-called "races."

Languages—there are about seventy language groups from which all modern languages have developed.

Archaeology—the presence of common building structures, like pyramids, around the world confirms the biblical account.

Literature—recorded and oral records tell of similar events relating to the Flood and the dispersion at Babel.

Christ

God did not leave mankind without a way to be redeemed from its sinful state. The Law was given to Moses to show how far away man is from God's standard of perfection. Rather than the sacrifices, which only covered sins, people needed a Savior to take away their sin. This was accomplished when Jesus Christ came to earth to live a perfect life and, by that obedience, was able to be the sacrifice to satisfy God's wrath for all who believe.

The deity of Christ and the amazing plan that was set forth before the foundation of the earth is the core of Christian doctrine. The earthly life of Jesus was the fulfillment of many prophecies and confirms the truthfulness of the Bible. His miracles and presence in human form demonstrate that God is both intimately concerned with His creation and able to control it in an absolute way.

Other contexts include:

Psychology—popular secular psychology teaches of the inherent goodness of man, but Christ has lived the only perfect life. Mankind needs a Savior to redeem it from its unrighteousness.

Biology—Christ's virgin birth demonstrates God's sovereignty over nature.

Physics—turning the water into wine and the feeding of the five thousand demonstrate Christ's deity and His sovereignty over nature.

History—time is marked (in the western world) based on the birth of Christ despite current efforts to change the meaning.

Art—much art is based on the life of Christ and many of the masters are known for these depictions, whether on canvas or in music.

Cross

Because God is perfectly just and holy, He must punish sin. The sinless life of Jesus Christ was offered as a substitutionary sacrifice for all of those who will repent and put their faith in the Savior. After His death on the Cross, He defeated death by rising on the third day and is now seated at the right hand of God.

The events surrounding the crucifixion and resurrection have a most significant place in the life of Christians.

Though there is no way to scientifically prove the resurrection, there is likewise no way to prove the stories of evolutionary history. These are matters of faith founded in the truth of God's Word and His character. The eyewitness testimony of over 500 people and the written Word of God provide the basis for our belief.

Other contexts include:

Biology—the biological details of the crucifixion can be studied alongside the anatomy of the human body.

History—the use of crucifixion as a method of punishment was short-lived in historical terms and not known at the time it was prophesied.

Art—the crucifixion and resurrection have inspired many wonderful works of art.

Consummation

God, in His great mercy, has promised that He will restore the earth to its original state—a world without death, suffering, war, and disease. The corruption introduced by Adam's sin will be removed. Those who have repented and put their trust in the completed work of Christ on the Cross will experience life in this new heaven and earth. We will be able to enjoy and worship God forever in a perfect place.

This future event is a little more difficult to connect with academic subjects. However, the hope of a life in God's presence and in the absence of sin can be inserted in discussions of human conflict, disease, suffering, and sin in general.

Other contexts include:

History—in discussions of war or human conflict the coming age offers hope.

Biology—the violent struggle for life seen in the predator-prey relationships will no longer taint the earth.

Medicine—while we struggle to find cures for diseases and alleviate the suffering of those enduring the effects of the Curse, we ultimately place our hope in the healing that will come in the eternal state.

The preceding examples are given to provide ideas for integrating the Seven C's of History into a broad range of curriculum activities. We would recommend that you give your students, and yourself, a better understanding of the Seven C's framework by using AiG's *Answers for Kids* curriculum. The first seven lessons of this curriculum cover the Seven C's and will establish a solid understanding of the true history, and future, of the universe. Full lesson plans, activities, and student resources are provided in the curriculum set.

We also offer bookmarks displaying the Seven C's and a wall chart. These can be used as visual cues for the students to help them recall the information and integrate new learning into its proper place in a biblical worldview.

Even if you use other curricula, you can still incorporate the Seven C's teaching into those. Using this approach will help students make firm connections between biblical events and every aspect of the world around them, and they will begin to develop a truly biblical worldview and not just add pieces of the Bible to what they learn in "the real world."

Mammals

1 The World of Animals

Is it a mouse or a moose?

Supply list

Note: Throughout this book you may wish to have additional resources with color pictures and information about each group of animals being studied. Animal encyclopedias or other resources, such as the Answers in Genesis *Zoo Guide* and *Aquarium Guide*, can be valuable in enhancing the lessons.

What did we learn?

- What are the two major divisions of animals? **Vertebrates and invertebrates.**
- What are two similarities among all animals? **They move and they must eat plants or other animals.**

Taking it further

- When did God create the different animal kinds? **On Day Five of creation God created fish and birds; on Day Six He created land animals. See Genesis 1.**
- How is man different from animals? **Humans have a conscience so they can tell right from wrong; animals act on instinct. People have a spirit so they can have a relationship with God; animals do not. People were made in God's image; animals were not. Despite our physical similarities, people are spiritually very different from animals. God gave man dominion over the animals. See Genesis 1:28.**

2 Vertebrates

Does it have a backbone?

Supply list

3-ring binder
12 or more dividers with tabs

Supplies for Challenge

Drawing materials

What did we learn?

- What are the two major divisions of the animal kingdom? **Vertebrates and invertebrates.**
- What characteristics define an animal as a vertebrate? **Vertebrates have a spinal cord ending in a brain protected by a backbone. They also have internal skeletons.**
- What are the five groups of vertebrates? **Mammals, birds, amphibians, reptiles, and fish.**

Taking it further

- Think about pictures you have seen of dinosaur skeletons. Do you think dinosaurs were vertebrates or invertebrates? Why do you think that? **Dinosaurs were vertebrates. This is shown by the fact that dinosaurs have internal skeletons and these skeletons contain vertebrae along the backs of the animals.**

3 Mammals

The fuzzy creatures

Supply list

Copy of "Mammals Have Fur" worksheet

Samples of hair from as many mammals as possible

Book showing pictures of different mammals

Suggestions for animal books: *Magnificent Mammals* by Buddy and Kay Davis, and *Kingfisher Illustrated Animal Encyclopedia*.

What did we learn?

- What five characteristics are common to all mammals? **They are warm-blooded, breathe with lungs, give birth to live young, nurse their young, and have hair or fur.**

- Why do mammals have hair? **To keep them warm, to aid in the sense of touch, and for some it provides camouflage.**

- Why is a platypus considered a mammal even though it lays eggs? **It nurses its young.**

Taking it further

- Name some ways that mammals regulate their body temperature. **Mammals cool down by sweating or pant-ing. They heat up by eating, exercising, or covering their bodies to keep warm.**

- What are some animals that have hair that helps them hide from their enemies? **Tigers and zebras have stripes that make them hard to see. Lions are the color of their surroundings.**

Challenge: Mammal Feet

Deer: **Unguligrade**

Rabbit: **Plantigrade**

Giraffe: **Unguligrade**

Wolf: **Digitigrade**

Skunk: **Plantigrade**

Elephant: **Unguligrade**

Opossum: **Plantigrade**

Chimpanzee: **Plantigrade**

Fox: **Digitigrade**

4 Mammals Large & Small

Armadillo to zebra

Supply list

Drawing paper

Markers, colored pencils, or paint

What did we learn?

- What is the largest land mammal? **Elephant.**

- What is the tallest land mammal? **Giraffe.**

- What do bears eat? **Nearly anything, but they prefer plants, roots, and berries.**

Taking it further

- What do you think is the most fascinating mammal? Why do you think that? **Answers will vary.**

5 Monkeys & Apes

Primates

Supply list

Copy of "Mammals Word Search"

Mammals Word Search

D	G	E	U	T	A	F	R	O	P	K	L	H	Y	U
B	E	N	D	R	**M**	L	J	I	O	S	C	X	F	A
A	**Z**	**E**	**B**	**R**	**A**	Z	C	V	B	C	A	B	S	R
M	N	I	D	S	**M**	**F**	V	G	F	**T**	T	J	**A**	E
S	R	E	I	H	**M**	**U**	X	A	**A**	I	**M**	U	**P**	U
C	O	L	S	**W**	**A**	**R**	**M**	**B**	**L**	**O**	**O**	**D**	**E**	**D**
C	**A**	**M**	**E**	**L**	R	H	O	P	T	W	**U**	P	E	A
K	E	Y	M	O	**Y**	U	S	**P**	Z	E	**S**	R	R	W
F	R	L	U	G	**G**	D	R	W	**R**	**G**	**E**	K	H	U
M	L	U	L	E	**L**	**I**	**V**	**E**	**B**	**I**	**R**	**T**	**H**	S
O	U	E	N	A	A	T	G	L	A	**R**	**M**	D	O	B
C	N	H	**M**	**O**	**N**	**K**	**E**	**Y**	V	A	I	A	N	P
F	**G**	Y	B	U	**D**	L	E	W	C	F	A	N	**T**	L
H	**S**	A	L	E	R	U	P	Q	Z	**F**	L	U	H	**E**
R	A	J	C	J	K	**W**	**H**	**A**	**L**	**E**	E	S	O	P

What did we learn?

- What are two common characteristics of all primates? **They have five fingers and five toes, and eyes on the fronts of their heads giving them binocular vision.**

- What are the three groups of primates? **Monkeys, apes, and prosimians.**
- What is one difference between apes and monkeys? **Apes do not have tails, monkeys do. Also, an ape's arms are longer than its legs, but this is not true for monkeys.**
- Where do New World Monkeys live? **In the western hemisphere.**
- Where do Old World Monkeys live? **In the eastern hemisphere.**
- What is a prehensile tail? **A tail that can grasp onto things.**

Taking it further

- If a monkey lives in South America is it likely to have a prehensile tail? **Yes, because New World Monkeys have prehensile tails and Old World Monkeys do not.**
- Are you more likely to find a monkey or an ape in a tree in the rain forest? **You are more likely to find a monkey in a tree. Many apes do not spend a lot of time in trees, whereas most monkeys live the majority of their lives in trees.**
- Why do most prosimians have very large eyes? **The majority of prosimians are nocturnal, that is, they sleep during the day and are awake at night. Large eyes allow these animals to see better at night.**

6 Aquatic Mammals

They live in the water?

Supply list

Toothbrush	2 cups
Stop watch	Water
Chopped nuts, fruits, or vegetables	

What did we learn?

- Why are dolphins and whales considered mammals and not fish? **They are warm-blooded, give birth to live young, nurse their babies and breathe air with lungs.**

- What is the main difference between the tails of fish and the tails of aquatic mammals? **Fish tails move from side to side and mammal tails, or flukes, move up and down.**
- What is another name for a manatee? **Sea cow.**
- Why are manatees sometimes called this? **They move slowly and graze on sea grass and other sea plants just like a cow grazing in a field.**

Taking it further

- How has God specially designed aquatic mammals for breathing air? **First, He gave them blowholes or nostrils on the tops of their heads so it is easy to breathe while still being in the water. Second, He designed them to be able to stay submerged for several minutes or even an hour at a time so they do not have to stay near** the surface. **God also gave them flukes to help them resurface quickly.**

- What do you think might be one of the first things a mother whale or dolphin must teach a newborn baby? **One of the first things the mother will do is push the baby toward the surface of the water so it can get its first breath.**

7 Marsupials

Pouched animals

Supply list

Plastic zipper bag

Glue

Tag board or cardboard

Scissors

Fake fur or felt

Construction paper

Supplies for Challenge

Copy of "Koala Fun Facts" worksheet

Book or internet sites on koalas

What did we learn?

- What is a marsupial? **An animal that gives birth to very tiny underdeveloped young. The young then spend the next several months developing in the mother's pouch.**

- Name at least three marsupials? **Some of the more common marsupials include kangaroos, koalas, opossums, numbats, and Tasmanian devils.**

- How has God designed the kangaroo for jumping? **A kangaroo has large powerful hind legs, large hind feet and long stretchy tendons that help conserve energy when hopping.**

Taking it further

- About half of a kangaroo's body weight is from muscle. This is nearly twice as much as in most animals its size. How might this fact contribute to its ability to hop? **Large muscles are needed to provide the strength to hop long distances. So a kangaroo has very large leg muscles.**

- How do you think a joey kangaroo keeps from falling out of its mother's pouch when she hops? **The nipple swells when the joey first attaches so it cannot slip off. Also, the pouch has muscles that can contract like a drawstring to keep the pouch closed.**

Koala Fun Facts

- We often hear a koala referred to as a koala bear, but it is not a bear. List three ways that a koala is different from a bear. **Koalas have pouches and give birth to very immature/undeveloped young; koalas only live in Australia; koalas live in trees and bears do not; koalas do not hibernate or sleep through the winter.**

- What is unusual about the koala's pouch? **It opens toward the back.**

- What does a baby koala eat? **Its mother's milk.**

- What does an adult koala eat? **Eucalyptus leaves.**

- What special design features make koalas able to eat this kind of food? **They have special grinding teeth, they have bacteria in their stomachs that help them digest the leaves.**

- How long does a baby koala spend in its mother's pouch? **6 months.**

- How does the mother koala carry her youngster after it leaves the pouch? **On her back.**

- What is special about the skin on the koala's feet that helps it to climb trees? **It is rough—friction skin—that grips even smooth trees.**

- What is special about the koala's hands that help it survive? **It has thumbs that grasp trees and leaves.**

- How much does a koala sleep? **Up to 20 hours a day.**

- About how much does an adult koala weigh? **19–33 pounds.**

- What is the average life span of a koala? **10–15 years.**

QUIZ 1

Mammals

Lessons 1–7

Short answer:

1. What are the two main groups of animals? **Vertebrates and invertebrates.**

2. What are the five major groups of vertebrates? **Mammals, birds, amphibians, reptiles, fish.**

3. What are five common characteristics of mammals? **Warm-blooded, breathe air with lungs, fur/hair, live birth, nurse young.**

4. What makes a marsupial different from other mammals? **Has a pouch.**

5. What makes a vertebrate unique? **Has a spinal cord ending in a brain, backbone.**

Mark each statement as either True or False.

6. _F_ Animals can produce their own food.

7. _F_ Dolphins are large fish.

8. _T_ Marsupials give birth to tiny live babies

9. _F_ Baleen whales have large teeth.

10. _F_ The elephant is the largest animal in the world. **Note: Elephants are the largest land animal, but blue whales are the largest animal on earth.**

11. _T_ Monkeys have tails, but apes do not.

12. _T_ Marsupials live primarily in Australia and Tasmania.

13. _T_ Some marsupials are meat-eating animals.

14. _T_ A lemur is a primate.

15. _F_ Primates have eyes on the sides of their heads.

Challenge questions

16. Draw a foot of a mammal to represent each of the following stances:

    Unguligrade: **Any animals with a hoof—horse, deer, or elephant.**

    Digitigrade: **Any animal that walks on its toes—dog, cat, wolf, or fox.**

    Plantigrade: **Any animal that walks on flat feet—rabbit, skunk, opossum, monkey, or bear.**

17. Match the parts of a ruminant's digestive system with its definition.

    _A_ Rumen   _E_ Abomasum

    _C_ Cud   _B_ Reticulum   _D_ Omasum

18. List three special design features that God gave whales. **Blowhole separate from mouth, ability to regulate temperature with fins, ability to regulate blood pressure/body pressure when diving, ability to shut down unnecessary functions while feeding, echolocation, ability to expand throat when eating.**

19. List three special design features that God gave koalas. **Ability to eat and digest leaves, special teeth, bacteria in stomach, friction skin on feet for climbing, thumbs for grasping, pouch for babies.**

20. Explain why an ape doing sign language does not necessarily support the evolution of man from apes. **Many animals have some level of intelligence, but none are close to humans. More importantly, humans have a spirit that relates to God. Sign language does not necessarily demonstrate humanity.**

Birds & Fish

8 Birds

Fine feathered friends

Supply list

Copy of "Bird Beaks" and ""Bird Feet" worksheets

Bird guides or encyclopedias

Supplies for Challenge

Animal or bird encyclopedias

What did we learn?

- How do birds differ from mammals? **Birds have feathers and wings, lay eggs, and usually can fly.**
- How are birds the same as mammals? **They are both warm-blooded and breathe with lungs.**

Taking it further

- How can you identify one bird from another? **By their size, shape, color of feathers, beak and feet shape, calls, and songs.**

- What birds can you identify near your home? **Use a field guide to help you.**
- Why might you see different birds near your home in the summer than in the winter? **Many birds migrate to live in a warmer area in the winter and a cooler area in the summer, so different birds may be in your area at different times of the year.**

Challenge: Birds vs. Reptiles

- List some characteristics that may vary among a species due to natural selection. Look through an animal encyclopedia to see examples of these characteristic. Notice that not one of these various characteristics has resulted in a new species. **Color, size and shape of beaks, size and shape of legs, size of body, coloring of feathers.**

9 Flight

How do those birds do that?

Supply list

Copy of "God Designed Birds to Fly" worksheet

1 or more bird feathers   Magnifying glass

God Designed Birds to Fly worksheet

- **Pictures should be similar to those in the student manual.**

What did we learn?

- What are some ways birds are designed for flight? **They have strong breast muscles, rigid backbones, hollow bones, efficient respiratory systems, feathers and wings.**
- What are the three kinds of bird feathers? **Down, contour, and flight feathers.**

- How does a bird repair a feather that is pulled open? **By preening—running the feather through its beak to re-hook the barbs.**
- How does a bird's tail work like a rudder? **It is moved from side to side to help steer.**

Taking it further

- Why can't man fly by strapping wings to his arms? **Man is not designed for flight. He does not have the strong breast muscles and stiff backbone needed. Humans are also too heavy to lift themselves with their arms.**

- How do you think birds use their feathers to stay warm? **Birds can fluff up their feathers and trap air under and between them. The heat from their bodies warms the trapped air, creating a barrier between their bodies and the cold air around them.**
- How is an airplane wing like a bird's wing? **They both have the same airfoil shape that allows the air flowing over the wing to create lift. Also, airplane wings are designed with the ability to change shape for different conditions, just like birds' wings.**

10 The Bird's Digestive System

They sure eat a lot.

Supply list

Copy of "God Designed the Bird's Digestive System" worksheet

Owl pellet (optional)

God Designed the Bird's Digestive System worksheet

- **See illustration in student manual.**

What did we learn?

- How does a bird "chew" its food without teeth? **God designed birds with an organ called a gizzard, which grinds the food up internally. In addition, some birds swallow small stones or pebbles that help to grind up the food as well.**

- What purposes does the crop serve? **It holds the food so a bird can eat quickly. It then releases the food to be digested in a constant stream to provide a more constant source of energy.**

Taking it further

- How is a bird's digestive system different from a human digestive system? **A bird has a crop and a gizzard; humans do not. A bird does not have a large intestine. A bird's digestive system digests food much more quickly.**
- How does a bird's digestive system help it to be a better flyer? **Because the food is digested quickly and efficiently, more energy is available for flying. Because the food is digested at a constant rate, a steady source of energy is provided for extended flying.**

11 Fish

Do fish go to school?

Supply list

Goldfish snack crackers   Glue

Paper   Colored pencils

What did we learn?

- What makes fish different from other animals? **They live in the water, are cold-blooded, and have gills and scales.**

- How do fish breathe? **They get oxygen from the water using gills.**

- Why do some sharks have to stay in motion? **They must have a constant flow of water over their gills to breathe, and the only way they can do that is to swim with their mouths open.**

- What is the difference between warm-blooded and cold-blooded animals? **Warm-blooded animals regulate their body temperature—it stays the same regardless of the surrounding temperature. Cold-blooded animals cannot regulate their body temperature—it goes up and down with the surrounding temperature.**

Taking it further

- Other than how they breathe, how are dolphins different from fish? **Dolphins are warm-blooded, give birth to live young, nurse their young, have hair, and do not have scales.**

- How are dolphins like fish? **They live in the water, swim, have fins and a tail, and eat fish.**

Challenge: Designed for Water

- Shape: **Fish that are flattened side to side can swim faster—slip through the water easily. Fish that are flattened top to bottom—can hide easily on the sea floor. Fish that are snake-like—can slip into crevices.**

- Scales: **Are an outgrowth of skin, arranged like shingles to provide protection, produce slime to fight fungus and allow for smoother movement through the water.**

- Color: **Fish are colored to blend into their environment, some can change their colors.**

- Gills: **efficiently remove oxygen from the water.**

- Eyes: **No eyelids, rigid lens that move forward and backward to focus, limited focusing is needed underwater.**

- Swim bladders: **Provide buoyancy.**

Fins & Other Fish Anatomy

Designed for efficiency

Supply list

Copy of "Fish Fins" worksheet

Construction paper   Glue

Scissors

Fish Fins worksheet

- **See illustration in student manual.**

What did we learn?

- What is the purpose of a swim bladder? **It gives the fish buoyancy. When it fills with air, it makes the fish lighter than the water, allowing it to rise. When the air is released, the fish becomes heavier than the water and it sinks. This buoyancy keeps the fish floating without having to keep moving its fins.**

- How did God design the fish to be such a good swimmer? **The shape of its body, its fins, and the mucus on its body all help it to be an efficient swimmer.**

Taking it further

- How does mucus make a fish a more efficient swimmer? **Since mucus is slippery, it reduces friction so the fish does not have to work as hard to move through the water. To see how this works, put your hand under some running water and watch how the water flows. Then, rub a little cooking oil on your hand and repeat the test. The water flows more quickly over your oily hand because there is less friction.**

- How has man used the idea of a swim bladder in his inventions? **Submarines use air to help keep them afloat at the desired depth. Also, life rafts fill with air to help them float to the top of the water.**

- What other function can fins have besides helping with swimming? **Fins can provide protection from predators. Fins can make it difficult for a predator to swallow a fish. In addition, some fins are shaped and colored to help provide camouflage.**

- What similar design did God give to both fish and birds to help them get where they are going? **They both have rudder-like tails that help them steer, and bodies specially shaped for moving through their environments.**

13 Cartilaginous Fish

No bones about it!

Supply list

Modeling clay

Supplies for Challenge

Pictures of cartilaginous fish

What did we learn?

- How do cartilaginous fish differ from bony fish? **Their skeletons are made from cartilage instead of bone. Also, many of these fish do not have the typical torpedo-shaped body.**

- Why is a lamprey called a parasite? **It does not eat prey. Instead, it attaches its mouth to a living animal, usually a fish, and sucks its blood for nutrients.**

- Why can sharks and stingrays be dangerous to humans? **Sharks can attack with their sharp teeth and stingrays can sting with their tails.**

Taking it further

- Why are shark babies born independent? **Like many other animals, sharks do not care for their young, so the babies must be able to care for themselves at birth. Many adult sharks will eat young sharks, so babies must avoid adults until they are large enough to defend themselves.**

- What do you think is the shark's biggest natural enemy? **Other sharks.**

QUIZ 2 Birds & Fish

Lessons 8–13

Short answer:

1. Look at each picture of birds' feet below. Below each picture write the term you think is most appropriate: **A. Water B. Bird of prey C. Perching D. Runner**

2. Look at each picture of birds' beaks below. Next to each picture write what you think that bird is likely to eat: **A. Seeds B. Water plants C. Other animals D. Nectar**

3. List three ways that birds were specially designed for flight. **Strong breast muscles, stiff backbone, hollow bones, efficient digestive and respiratory systems, and feathers.**

4. List two special design features of a bird's digestive system. **It is very fast and efficient, crop releases food at a constant rate, and gizzard grinds food.**

5. Name three kinds of fins found on most fish. **Pectoral, pelvic, dorsal, anal, caudal.**

6. Name two kinds of cartilaginous fish. **Sharks, rays, hagfish, and lampreys.**

Challenge questions

Mark each statement as either True or False.

7. _T_ Animals can adapt to changes in their surroundings.

8. _F_ Birds evolved from reptiles.

9. _F_ Birds and reptiles are both cold-blooded animals.

10. _T_ Scales are very different from feathers.

11. _T_ There can be great variety among species.

12. _F_ Flightless birds have useless wings.

13. _T_ Kiwi birds lay eggs that are very large compared to their body size.

14. _T_ Penguins only live in the southern hemisphere.

15. _T_ Birds have a very efficient respiratory system.

16. _F_ Birds have a bellows type of respiratory system.

17. _T_ Fish scales fit together smoothly from head to tail.

18. _T_ Some fish can sense things that other animals cannot.

19. _F_ Fish have very small olfactory lobes compared to their brain size.

20. _T_ There are over 600 species of cartilaginous fish.

Unit 3
Amphibians & Reptiles

14 Amphibians

Air or water?

No Supplies

What did we learn?

- What are the characteristics that make amphibians unique? **They spend part of their lives in water breathing with gills, and part of their lives on land breathing with lungs. They are also cold-blooded, usually have smooth moist skin and lay eggs.**

- How can you tell a frog from a toad? **In general, frogs have smooth moist skin, while toads have dry bumpy skin.**

- How can you tell a salamander from a lizard? **Salamanders have smooth skin and lizards have dry scales on their skin. Also, salamanders go through a larval stage but lizards do not.**

Taking it further

- What advantages do cold-blooded animals have over warm-blooded animals? **They don't have to eat as often and can usually survive a broader range of temperatures.**

- What advantages do warm-blooded animals have over cold-blooded animals? **Cold-blooded animals' activities are more restricted by temperature extremes. A warm-blooded animal can still be quite active in very cold or very warm weather.**

- Why are most people unfamiliar with caecilians? **Caecilians spend most of their time underground and live only in tropical rain forests, so most people never see them.**

15 Amphibian Metamorphosis

Making a change

Supply list

Copy of "Amphibian Life Cycle" worksheet

Tadpoles (optional)   Food for raising a frog

Tank

Amphibian Life Cycle worksheet

- **See illustrations in student manual.**

What did we learn?

- Describe the stages an amphibian goes through in its life cycle. **It begins as an egg, and then it hatches into a** larva. In a frog, this is the tadpole stage. Then, it slowly changes into an adult. This is the metamorphosis stage in which lungs develop and gills disappear, and the creature changes its shape from a water dweller without legs to a land dweller with legs.

- What are gills? **They are special organs on the sides of water animals that extract oxygen from the water as water passes over or through them.**

- What are lungs? **They are special organs that extract oxygen from the air as air passes through them.**

Taking it further

- Does the amphibian lifecycle represent molecules-to-man evolution? Why or why not? **NO! Evolution says that one kind of animal changes into another.**

A frog is still a frog even when it is a tadpole. A tadpole always changes into a frog. It does not grow up to be a bird or a mammal or even a salamander. It is always what God made it to be, even if its infant form is significantly different from its adult form.

16 Reptiles

Scaly animals

Supply list

Paper	Sequins or flat beads
Pictures of reptiles	Glue

What did we learn?

- What makes reptiles different from amphibians? **Reptiles have scales and amphibians do not. Also, reptiles have lungs all their lives and do not go through metamorphosis.**
- What are the four groups of reptiles? **Lizards, snakes, turtles, and crocodiles.**

Taking it further

- How do reptiles keep from overheating? **They stay in the shade or other cooler places during the hottest part of the day. Many sleep during the day and are only active at night.**
- What would a reptile likely do if you dug it out of its winter hibernation spot? **It would appear dead. It would not move or eat. If you brought it inside and it warmed up, then it would seem to come alive, though it is actually alive even in its hibernating state.**

17 Snakes

Those hissing, slithering creatures

Supply list

An open area on the floor for moving about

What did we learn?

- How are snakes different from other reptiles? **They have no legs.**
- What are the three groups of snakes? **Constrictors, colubrids, and venomous snakes.**
- How is a snake's sense of smell different from that of most other animals? **It uses its tongue to collect scent particles, and then touches them to an organ called the Jacobson's organ inside its mouth.**
- What is unique about how a snake eats? **It swallows its food whole and can eat something larger than its body diameter by unhooking its jaw and stretching its mouth very wide.**

Taking it further

- How are small snakes different from worms? **Snakes have backbones, scales, and well-developed eyes. Worms do not have any of these. Also, snakes have much more complicated internal systems.**
- If you see a snake in your yard, how do you know if it is dangerous? **You should learn to identify snakes using a guidebook or other resource. Unless you have your parent's permission, you should never approach a snake.**

18 Lizards

Chameleons and Gila monsters

Supply list

Paper   Face paint
Markers, colored pencils or paints

What did we learn?

- List three ways a lizard might protect itself from a predator. **It could change its color, crawl into a crack in a rock and inflate its body, or break off its tail to escape.**
- What do lizards eat? **Mostly insects; some eat plants and others eat dead animals.**

Taking it further

- Horny lizards are short compared to many other lizards and are often called horny toads. What distinguishes a lizard from a toad? **Lizards are reptiles, toads are amphibians. Toads do not have scales but lizards do. Also, lizards do not have gills when they are young, nor do they experience metamorphosis, but toads do.**
- Why might some people like having lizards around? **They eat insects and do not harm people.**
- How does changing color protect a lizard? **It makes it hard for the predator to see it.**
- What other reasons might cause a lizard to change colors? **To attract a mate or scare off competitors. Chameleons often use their coloring to communicate with other chameleons.**

19 Turtles & Crocodiles

Turtle or tortoise, crocodile or alligator—how do you tell?

Supply list

Copy of "How Can You Tell Them Apart?" worksheet
Tape (cloth or first aid tape is best)
Sink

How Can You Tell Them Apart? worksheet

- **Student drawings should be similar to pictures in student manual.**

What did we learn?

- Where do turtles usually live? **In the water.**
- Where do tortoises usually live? **On land.**
- How does the mother crocodile carry her eggs to the water? **In her mouth.**
- Why can't you take a turtle out of its shell? **Its shell is part of its body.**
- How do crocodiles stalk their prey? **They float in the water, wait for prey to approach and then clamp their jaws around the prey and drag it under the water to drown it before eating it.**

Taking it further

- Why might it be difficult to see a crocodile? **When it is floating in the water, it looks very much like a fallen log. This is how it tricks its prey into coming close enough to be eaten.**

QUIZ 3

Amphibians & Reptiles

Lessons 14–19

1. What defines an animal as a vertebrate? **Vertebrates have backbones with a spine along the back ending in a brain.**

Place the letters of the characteristics that apply next to each animal group.

2. Mammals: **A, C, G, J, L, (H for some)**

3. Birds: **A, E, H, J, M**

4. Fish: **B, D, H, K, N, (G for a few)**

5. Reptiles: **B, D, H, J**

6. Amphibians: **B, F, H, I , J, K**

Challenge questions

Fill in the blank with the correct term from below.

7. Amphibians communicate primarily by **_sound_**.

8. Male frogs have inflatable **_air sacs_** for communication.

9. Each frog species communicates on a different **_frequency_**.

10. The Surinam toad presses eggs into the mother's **_back_**.

11. The midwife toad carries eggs strapped to its **_legs_**.

12. The mouth brooding frog carries its tadpoles in its **_mouth/air sacs_**.

13. A **_triceratops_** is a ceratopsian dinosaur.

14. An **_allosaurus_** is a theropod dinosaur.

15. An **_apatosaurus_** is a sauropod dinosaur.

16. Marine iguanas are well adapted to life in and near the **_water_**.

17. The **_carapace_** is the top part of the turtle's shell.

18. The **_plastron_** is the bottom part of the turtle's shell.

19. Manta rays eat **_plankton_**.

20. Baby manta rays are called **_pups_**.

Unit 4
Arthropods

20 Invertebrates

Creatures without a backbone

Supply list

A good imagination

White board with markers (optional)

What did we learn?

- What are some differences between vertebrates and invertebrates? **The main difference is that vertebrates have backbones that protect their spinal cords. Invertebrates do not have backbones or spinal cords. Also, vertebrates have internal skeletons and invertebrates don't.**

- What are the six categories of invertebrates? **Arthropods, mollusks, cnidarians, echinoderms, sponges, and worms.**

Taking it further

- Why might we think that there are more vertebrates than invertebrates in the world? **We don't notice invertebrates as much as we do vertebrates. Invertebrates are usually small, a great many are microscopic, and so we just don't see them as often. Also, many invertebrates live in the water, so, again, we don't see them very often.**

21 Arthropods

Invertebrates with jointed feet

Supply list

Copy of the "Arthropod Pie Chart"

Supplies for Challenge

| Balloons | String |
| Newspaper | Flour |

Arthropod Pie Chart

_A_ Insects	_E_ Centipedes
_C_ Crustaceans	_D_ Millipedes
_B_ Arachnids	

What did we learn?

- What do all arthropods have in common? **They are invertebrates [no backbone] with jointed feet, segmented bodies, and exoskeletons.**

- What is the largest group of arthropods? **Insects, with over 1 million species.**

Taking it further

- How are endoskeletons (internal) and exoskeletons (external) similar? **They both provide support and protection for the body. They help give the animal its form and shape.**

- How are endoskeletons and exoskeletons different? **Endoskeletons are on the inside of the body and are usually made of bone or cartilage. Also, endoskeletons grow as the body grows. Exoskeletons are on the outside of the body and are made from chitin, a substance similar to starch. Exoskeletons do not grow with the animal and must be shed and replaced periodically as the body grows.**

- Why should you be cautious when hunting for arthropods? **Many arthropods are poisonous, including some spiders, scorpions, and centipedes.**

22 Insects

Don't let them bug you.

Supply list

Copy of "Water Skipper Pattern"

Paint	Scissors
Bowl of water	2 toothpicks per child
3 Styrofoam balls per child	Paper
4 pipe cleaners per child	Tape
1 index card per child	

What did we learn?

- What characteristics classify an animal as an insect? **Insects are invertebrates with jointed feet, 3 body parts** [head, thorax, and abdomen], 6 legs, antennae, and usually havie wings.

- How can insects be harmful to humans? **They can destroy crops and spread disease.**

- How can insects be helpful? **Some insects eat other insects. For example, dragonflies eat mosquitoes, and ladybugs eat aphids. Many insects pollinate flowers. Other insects provide food for many other animals.**

Taking it further

- How might insects make noise? **Some insects make noise by flapping their wings. Others, like crickets, rub their legs together to make noises.**

23 Insect Metamorphosis

Making a change

Supply list

Copy of "Stages of Metamorphosis" worksheet

Butterfly larvae and habitat (optional)

Stages of Metamorphosis worksheet

- **See student manual.**

What did we learn?

- What are the three stages of incomplete metamorphosis? **Egg, nymph, and adult.**

- What are the four stages of complete metamorphosis? **Egg, larva, chrysalis (or pupa), and adult.**

Taking it further

- What must an adult insect look for when trying to find a place to lay her eggs? **The eggs must be laid on a plant that the larva can eat. A larva spends most of its time eating and cannot search for food, so food must be readily available.**

24 Arachnids

Spiders and such

Supply list

Required activity:

Several large and small marshmallows for each child

Flexible wire (about 4 inches for each child)

1 toothpick per child

4–6 pipe cleaners per child

First optional activity:

Peanut butter

2 raisins per child

2 round crackers per child

8 pretzel sticks per child

Second optional activity:

Spider webs

Magnifying glass

Powdered sugar

What did we learn?

- How do arachnids differ from insects? **Arachnids have only two body parts (cephalothorax and abdomen), eight legs, no wings or antennae, and many spin webs.**

- Why are ticks and mites called parasites? **They feed off of living hosts.**

Taking it further

- Why don't spiders get caught in their own webs? **Only some of the web strands are sticky. The spider walks on the ones that are not sticky. Also, spiders secrete an oily substance that coats their feet and keeps them from sticking to their own webs.**

25 Crustaceans

Are they crusty?

Supply list

Modeling clay

Magnifying glass for optional activity

Supplies for Challenge

Research materials on crustaceans

What did we learn?

- What do all crustaceans have in common? **They have jointed legs, exoskeletons, two body sections, two pairs of antennae, and two or more pairs of legs and gills.**

- What are some ways that the crayfish is specially designed for its environment? **It has claws for defense and for eating. Its mouth is on the underside of its body, making it easier to eat food from the bottom of the river.**

Taking it further

- Why might darting backward be a good defense for the crayfish? **It is unexpected and can confuse an enemy.**

- At first glance, scorpions and crayfish (or crawdads) look a lot alike. How does a scorpion differ from a crayfish? **A scorpion lives on land and has eight legs, a stinger, and no antennae. Crayfish live in the water and have ten legs, antennae, and no stingers.**

- How can something as large as a blue whale survive by eating only tiny crustaceans? **It eats lots and lots of them—up to 8,000 pounds (3,600 kg) per day!**

- If you want to observe crustaceans, what equipment might you need? **Jar, net, microscope or magnifying glass, and a trap.**

26 Myriapods

How many shoes would a centipede have to buy?

Supply list

A good memory and a sense of adventure

(A baseball cap might be fun, too.)

Supplies for Challenge

Modeling clay

Pipe cleaners or craft wire

What did we learn?

- How can you tell a centipede from a millipede? **Centipedes are usually smaller, flatter and have longer antennae. Also, centipedes have 1 pair of legs per body segment while millipedes have 2 pairs per segment.**
- What are the five groups of arthropods? **Insects, arachnids, crustaceans, centipedes, and millipedes.**
- What do all arthropods have in common? **They have jointed legs, exoskeletons, and 2 or more body regions.**

Taking it further

- What are some common places you might find arthropods? **Nearly everywhere!**
- Arthropods are supposed to live outside, but sometimes they get into our homes. What arthropods have you seen in your home? **Ants, flies, mosquitoes, spiders, etc..**

Arthropods

Lessons 20–26

Write Yes if the creature below is an arthropod, write No if it is not.

1. _**Yes**_ ant
2. _**Yes**_ tick
3. _**No**_ trout
4. _**Yes**_ spider
5. _**Yes**_ scorpion
6. _**Yes**_ crab
7. _**Yes**_ cricket
8. _**Yes**_ butterfly
9. _**No**_ clam
10. _**No**_ mouse
11. _**Yes**_ centipede
12. _**No**_ snail
13. _**Yes**_ roly-poly
14. _**Yes**_ crawdad
15. _**No**_ starfish
16. _**No**_ lizard

17. What are the four stages of complete metamorphosis for an insect? **egg, larva, chrysalis (or pupa), adult**

Fill in the blanks with the appropriate numbers.

18. An insect has _**3**_ body parts, _**6**_ legs, _**2**_ antennae and _**2 or 4**_ wings.
19. A spider has _**2**_ body parts, _**8**_ legs, _**0**_ antennae and _**0**_ wings.
20. A centipede has _**1**_ pair(s) of legs per body segment and a millipede has _**2**_ pair(s) of legs per body segment.

Challenge questions

Short answer:

21. Explain the purpose of an arthropod's exoskeleton. **The exoskeleton provides protection, keeps the animal from drying out, gives it form.**

22. What is the main ingredient in an exoskeleton? **Starch or chitin.**
23. Identify which segment (head, thorax, abdomen) is primarily responsible for each of the following functions in insects.
    Locomotion: **Thorax**
    Internal functions: **Abdomen**
    Sensory input: **Head**
24. What are two purposes of bioluminescence in fireflies? **Protection from enemies, finding a mate.**
25. Do male or female tarantulas live longer? **Female.**
26. What do tarantulas usually eat? **Grasshoppers, crickets, and other small animals.**
27. List three types of symmetry commonly found among animals. **Bilateral, radial, spherical.**
28. What does it mean if an animal is asymmetrical? **It has no symmetry; it cannot be divided into similar halves.**
29. How does a millipede protect itself from predators? **It coils up, produces smelly or caustic liquid.**
30. Which is more dangerous, a centipede or a millipede? **A centipede is poisonous.**

Unit 5
Other Invertebrates

27 Mollusks

Creatures with shells

Supply list

Several sea shells Shell identification guide

Supplies for Challenge

Balloon

What did we learn?

- What are three groups of mollusks? **Bivalves, gastropods, and cephalopods.**
- What body structures do all mollusks have? **They all have soft bodies, a muscular foot, a hump for internal organs and a mantle that forms a shell in most species.**

- How can you use a shell to help identify an animal? **The size, shape and coloring of each shell are unique to its species. Some shells spiral counter-clockwise and others spiral clockwise. Some are two pieces and some are only one piece.**

Taking it further

- How are pearls formed? **Any irritant that gets inside an oyster's shell is coated with a pearly substance over and over again. After a period of several years, it is large enough to be of value to people. To speed up this process, many oyster farmers now "seed" oysters by placing hard round objects that are nearly the size of a pearl inside oyster shells. After only a few months, these artificial pearls are ready for harvesting.**

28 Cnidarians

Jellyfish, coral, and sea anemones

Supply list

Copy of "Coral Pattern" worksheet

Baking dish Salt

Thin cardboard Food coloring

Ammonia

Liquid bluing (located with laundry soap in grocery store)

Supplies for Challenge

Live hydra specimens (Optional—can be ordered from a science supply store)

What did we learn?

- What characteristics do all cnidarians share? **They have hollow bodies with stinging tentacles.**
- What are the three most common cnidarians? **Jellyfish, corals, and sea anemones.**

Taking it further

- How do you think some creatures are able to live closely with jellyfish? Accept reasonable answers. **Some animals have a tough skin or exoskeleton that protects them from jellyfish stings. Others have a special coating on their skin that protects them.**

- Why do you think an adult jellyfish is called a medusa? **The Medusa was a mythological creature with snakes for hair. A jellyfish, with all of its tentacles, resembles this creature.**
- Jellyfish and coral sometimes have symbiotic relationships with other creatures. What other symbiotic relationships can you name? **Some birds eat insects off of cattle. This feeds the birds and helps the cattle stay healthy. Also, lichen, that green and yellow scaly-looking substance on rocks, is actually fungus and algae living in a symbiotic relationship. The algae have chlorophyll and produce the food, while the fungus provides water, nutrients and protection. It is a beneficial relationship for both organisms.**

Challenge: Man O' War

- **Hydras can reproduce several different ways. They can reproduce by a process called budding where a new hydra forms from the side of the parent and then splits off. Hydras can also reproduce by sperm and eggs. Some species are able to produce both sperm and eggs from one animal. Other species have distinct male and female versions.**

29 Echinoderms

Spiny-skinned creatures

Supply list

Salt dough (1 cup salt, 1 cup flour, water to make a stiff dough)

Tag board or cardboard   Mini-chocolate chips

If possible: a real (dead) starfish or sand dollar (sometimes available at craft stores)

Supplies for Challenge

(optional): A preserved starfish for dissection

Plastic gloves   Dissecting tray and scalpel

What did we learn?

- What are three common echinoderms? **Starfish (sea stars), sand dollars, and sea urchins.**

- What do echinoderms have in common? **They all have spiky skin and most have 5 body parts radiating from a central disk.**

Taking it further

- Why would oyster and clam fishermen not want starfish in their oyster and clam beds? **Starfish can eat up to a dozen clams or oysters a day. This hurts the fishermen's business.**

- What would happen if the fishermen caught and cut up the starfish and then threw them back? **The starfish would regenerate resulting in more starfish. This happened in one fishing village. The fishermen thought they were getting rid of the starfish by cutting them in half, but actually ended up making many more of them.**

- What purpose might the spikes serve on echinoderms? **Most spikes are used for protection from predators.**

30 Sponges

How much water can a sponge hold?

Supply list

Synthetic sponges (and if possible, a real sea sponge)

Paper   Scissors

Tempera paints

What did we learn?

- How does a sponge eat? **Nutrients are absorbed from the water as it passes through the body of the sponge.**

- How does a sponge reproduce? **A sponge can reproduce by releasing eggs or a sponge can regenerate to** form new sponges from pieces that are cut or broken off of the original sponge.

- Why is a sponge an animal and not a plant? **A sponge cannot produce its own food and it reproduces with eggs so it is an animal.**

Taking it further

- Why can a sponge kill a coral colony? **It is immune to the poison darts of the coral.**
- What uses are there for sponges? **They are sometimes used for cleaning. But mostly they are used for sponge painting and other artwork.**
- Why are synthetic sponges more popular than real sponges? **They are much less expensive.**

31 Worms

Creepy crawlers

Supply list

Gummy worms	Rocks
Dirt	Crushed chocolate cookies
Dried leaves	Instant chocolate pudding

Supplies for Challenge

Paper	Drawing materials
Paint	

What did we learn?

- What kinds of worms are beneficial to man? **Segmented worms such as earthworms.**

- How are they beneficial? **They break down dead plant material, and can be used as fishing bait.**
- What kinds of worms are harmful? **Most other kinds of worms are parasitic and thus are harmful to their hosts; whether they are human or animal hosts.**

Taking it further

- How can you avoid parasitic worms? **Parasitic worms thrive in unsanitary conditions and are much more of a threat in undeveloped countries. Washing hands and raw vegetables and cooking meat well will help you avoid most parasites.**

QUIZ 5 Other Invertebrates

Lessons 27–31

Mark each statement as either True or False.

1. _F_ All mollusks have visible shells.
2. _T_ A bivalve has two parts to its shell.
3. _T_ You can identify a mollusk by the shape of its shell.
4. _F_ The octopus is considered one of the least intelligent invertebrates.
5. _T_ Cnidarians usually experience a polyp stage sometime in their lifecycle.
6. _T_ Coral and algae have a symbiotic relationship.
7. _F_ Echinoderms are usually very dark colors.

8. _T_ Several invertebrates have the ability to regenerate.
9. _F_ Echinoderms have smooth skin.
10. _T_ A sponge is one of the simplest invertebrates.
11. _T_ Sponges can reproduce by eggs.
12. _F_ All worms are harmful to humans.

Short answer:

13. What do jellyfish, coral and sea anemones have in common? **They all have hollow bodies and stinging tentacles at least during part of their lifecycles.**
14. Name three groups of worms. **Segmented, flat, round.**

15. What part of the mollusk secretes its shell? **Mantle.**

16. Which kind of mollusk has only one part to its shell? **Gastropod.**

17. What is an adult jellyfish called? **Medusa.**

18. What is the name of the fertilizer produced by earthworms? **Compost.**

Challenge questions

Short answer:

19. Explain how cephalopods move. **Jet propulsion—suck in water then force it out the back.**

20. How can a nautilus remain buoyant as its shell gets bigger and heavier? **It fills inner chambers with gas/air.**

21. What is a siphonophore? **A collection of cnidarians living together in a symbiotic relationship.**

22. Name a common siphonophore. **Portuguese Man-of-War, by-the-wind sailor.**

23. What is a sieve plate in a starfish? **The openings that allow water into the starfish's water vascular system.**

24. What technology is being improved by the study of the Venus Flower Basket sponge? **Fiber optics.**

25. What is the name of the process that provides food for tubeworms? **Chemosynthesis.**

Simple Organisms

32 Kingdom Protista

Simple creatures?

Supply list

Colored pencils, markers, or crayons

Construction paper	Glue
Yarn	Optional: Microscope
Shoe	Pond water
Scissors	Slides

What did we learn?

- How are protists different from animals? **They consist of only one cell. Some contain chlorophyll.**

- How are they the same? **Protists reproduce, eat, move, grow and need oxygen just like other animals. Also, protists have all the same cell parts as other animal cells.**

Taking it further

- Why is a euglena a puzzle to scientists? **It has plant and animal characteristics.**

- Why are single-celled creatures not as simple as you might expect? **Just because there is only one cell does not mean it is simple. Single-celled creatures perform very complex functions. Most protists are more complex than any cell in the human body because human cells are more specialized and protist cells must perform more functions. Even the smallest organism demonstrates God's marvelous powers of design, and refutes the idea that life evolved on its own.**

33 Kingdom Monera & Viruses

Good and bad germs

Supply list

Hand soap and other anti-bacterial items in your house

What did we learn?

- How are bacteria similar to plants and animals? **They have cells, reproduce, and some can produce their own food.**

- How are bacteria different from plant and animal cells? **They do not have a defined nucleus.**

- How are viruses similar to plants and animals? **They have genetic information—DNA.**

- How are viruses different? **They do not reproduce on their own. They do not eat or grow in a normal sort of way.**

Taking it further

- Answer the following questions to test if a virus is alive.

  Does it have cells? **No.**

  Can it reproduce? **Only with the help of a host cell .**

  Is it growing? **Not in the ordinary sense of the word.**

  Does it move or respond to its environment? **Yes.**

Does it need food and water? **It needs host cells that use food and water. It is unclear if the viruses use these things directly.**

Does it have respiration? **No.**

Is it alive? **No, it does not have all of the requirements for biological life.**

- How can use of antibiotics be bad? **Antibiotics kill bacteria, but they cannot distinguish between good and bad bacteria. Overuse of antibiotics can kill too many of the good bacteria in your intestines and cause problems. Also, antibiotics kill most of the bad bacteria but some are resistant and do not die. These bacteria are the ones that survive and reproduce. The next generation of bacteria is not as easily killed by the antibiotics. Doctors are beginning to see diseases that used to respond to certain antibiotics no longer respond and must now be treated with stronger medicines. So we need to carefully use antibiotics when necessary, but not overuse them or use them incorrectly.**

QUIZ 6 Simple Organisms

Lessons 32–33

Match the parts of a cell to its function.

1. _E_ Nucleus
2. _C_ Cell membrane
3. _B_ Cytoplasm
4. _A_ Mitochondria
5. _D_ Vacuole

Match the single-celled organism with its description.

6. _C_ Flagellate
7. _A_ Sarcodine
8. _B_ Ciliate
9. _E_ Bacteria
10. _D_ Virus

Challenge questions

Mark each statement as either True or False.

11. _F_ Sporozoans have a very simple lifecycle.
12. _T_ Sporozoans reproduce asexually and sexually.
13. _T_ Sporozoans are parasites.
14. _T_ Plasmodium is a dangerous protist.
15. _F_ Antibiotic-resistant bacteria prove evolution.
16. _F_ Survival of the fittest is the same as evolution.
17. _T_ Fossilized bacteria are very similar to modern bacteria.
18. _T_ Bacteria support biblical creation.

34 Animal Notebook

Putting the animals together

Final Project supply list

Paper   Art supplies
Clip-art or other animal pictures
Worksheets from previous lessons
Photographs of projects from previous lessons

What did we learn?

- What do all animals have in common? **They are alive, they reproduce, they do not make their own food, they can move about during at least part of their life.**
- What is the difference between vertebrates and invertebrates? **Vertebrates have a backbone and invertebrates do not.**

- What sets protists apart from all the other animals? **They are single-celled creatures. Some, like the euglena, can make their own food.**

Taking it further

- What are some of the greatest or most interesting things you learned from your study of the world of animals? **Answers will vary.**
- What would you like to learn more about? **Check out books from the library to learn more.**

World of Animals

Lessons 1–34

Match each animal group with its unique characteristic.

1. _D_ Mammals
2. _G_ Birds
3. _A_ Fish
4. _F_ Reptiles
5. _H_ Amphibians
6. _B_ Arthropods
7. _C_ Mollusks
8. _I_ Echinoderms
9. _J_ Cnidarians
10. _E_ Protists

Define the following terms.

11. Invertebrate: **Animal without a backbone.**
12. Vertebrate: **Animal with a backbone.**
13. Cold-blooded animal: **Cold-blooded animals cannot regulate their body temperature; it is the same as the surrounding temperature.**
14. Warm-blooded animal: **Warm-blooded animals regulate their body temperature to keep it the same regardless of the surrounding temperature.**
15. Moneran: **Monerans are bacteria. They are single-celled organisms without a nucleus.**

Describe how a bird's feet are suited for each task listed below.

16. Swimming in a lake: **Webbed feet for paddling.**
17. Perching in a tree: **Three toes facing forward, one toe facing backward for grasping tree branches.**
18. Hunting prey: **Sharp claws (or talons) for grasping prey.**

Short answer:

19. Describe how a bird is specially designed for flight. **Birds have hollow bones, air-foil shaped wings, contour feathers that point toward the back of the body, special flight feathers, a tail that works like a rudder, and very efficient respiratory and circulatory systems.**
20. Name the three body parts of an insect. **Head, thorax, abdomen**
21. Name the two body parts of a spider. **Cephalothorax, abdomen**

Mark each statement as either True or False.

22. _T_ Snakes have a special organ for sensing smell.
23. _T_ Cold-blooded animals do not need to eat as often as warm-blooded animals.
24. _F_ Turtles can safely be removed from their shells.
25. _T_ Cartilaginous fish do not have any bones.
26. _T_ Centipedes are arthropods.
27. _F_ All crustaceans live in the water.
28. _T_ Insects are the most common arthropod.
29. _T_ Some creatures can live closely with jellyfish.
30. _F_ The best way to kill a starfish is to cut it in half.

Challenge questions

Match the term with its definition.

31. _B_ Unguligrade
32. _D_ Digitigrade
33. _E_ Plantigrade
34. _A_ Rumen
35. _G_ Abomasum
36. _C_ Reticulum
37. _F_ Omasum

Mark each statement as either True or False.

38. _F_ Darwin's finches prove evolution.
39. _T_ Birds have very efficient respiratory systems.
40. _T_ Fish sense food by smelling the water.
41. _F_ Frogs often confuse one species' call for another.
42. _T_ The largest dinosaurs were the sauropods.
43. _T_ Marine iguanas live only in the Galapagos Islands.
44. _F_ The plastron is the top of a turtle's shell.

45. _T_ A turtle's shell is made of the same material as fingernails.

Short answer:

46. Exoskeletons are made from _**chitin/starch**_.

47. The legs of an insect are attached to the _**thorax/middle**_ section of its body.

48. Bioluminescence causes an animal to _**glow**_.

49. Tarantulas have barbed _**hairs**_ that they kick at their enemies.

50. A _**nautilus, octopus, squid, cephalopod**_ moves through the water using jet propulsion.

51. Biomimetics is the study of animals to apply designs to _**human technology**_.

52. Tubeworms live near _**hydrothermal vents**_.

53. Plasmodium causes the disease _**malaria**_.

54. _**Antibiotics**_ are used to treat bacterial infections.

55. The stomach of a _**mosquito**_ is needed to complete the sexual reproduction of the plasmodium sporozoan.

35 Conclusion

Reflecting on the world of animals

Supply list

Bible

Paper and pencil

Resource Guide

Many of the following titles are available from Answers in Genesis (www.AnswersBookstore.com).

Suggested Books

Breathtaking Birds by Buddy and Kay Davis—Animal encyclopedia from a creation perspective

Magnificent Mammals by Buddy and Kay Davis—Animal encyclopedia from a creation perspective

Sensational Sea Creatures by Buddy and Kay Davis—Animal encyclopedia from a creation perspective

Reader's Digest North American Wildlife—A great resource to have for any field trip

Mammals Scholastic Voyages of Discovery by Scholastic Books—Interactive fun

Birds by Carolyn Boulton—Lots of suggested activities, good pictures

Play and Find Out About Bugs by Janice VanCleave—Great experiments

Jellyfish by Leighton Taylor—Good explanation of life cycle, great pictures

Zoo Guide by Answers in Genesis—A guide to over 100 animals from a creationist perspective

Aquarium Guide by Answers in Genesis—Take it to the aquarium with you

Museum Guide by Answers in Genesis—Take it to the natural history museum with you

God Created Series by Earl and Bonita Snellenberger—Coloring and sticker books that present God's creation to young children

Suggested Videos

Newton's Workshop by Moody Institute—Excellent Christian science series

Incredible Creatures that Defy Evolution Three volumes by Exploration Films—Learn about amazing design features

Exploring the Wildlife Kingdom by Exploration Films—Evolution free nature videos

Life's Story by NPN Videos—Shows how the interactions among living things could not have happened through evolution

We highly recommend purchasing one or more of the following to supplement the activities in this book:

Owl pellets
Frog habitat
Butterfly habitat
Dissection supplies

Field Trip Ideas

- Creation Museum in Petersburg, KY
- Farm or dairy
- Zoo, aquarium, or butterfly museum
- Fish hatchery
- Wildlife area

Creation Science Resources

Answers Book for Kids Four volumes by Ken Ham with Cindy Malott—Answers children's frequently asked questions

The New Answers Books 1 & 2 by Ken Ham and others—Answers frequently asked questions

Dinosaurs by Design by Duane T. Gish—All about dinosaurs and where they fit into creation

The Amazing Story of Creation by Duane T. Gish—Scientific evidence for the creation story

Creation Science by Felice Gerwitz and Jill Whitlock—Unit study focusing on creation

Creation: Facts of Life by Gary Parker—In-depth comparison of the evidence for creation and evolution

Dinosaurs for Kids by Ken Ham—Learn the true history of dinosaurs

Master Supply List

The following table lists all the supplies used for *God's Design for Life: World of Animals* activities. You will need to look up the individual lessons in the student book to obtain the specific details for the individual activities (such as quantity, color, etc.). The letter *c* denotes that the lesson number refers to the challenge activity. Common supplies such as colored pencils, construction paper, markers, scissors, tape, etc., are not listed.

Supplies needed (see lessons for details)	Lesson
3-ring binder	2
Ammonia	28
Baking dish	28
Balloons	21c, 27c
Bible	35
Bird feeder (optional)	8
Butterfly larvae (caterpillars)	23
Chocolate chips (mini size)	29
Dissection kit	29c
Dividers with tabs (12 or 13 per student)	2
Encyclopedia (animal)	all
Face paint	18
Fake fur or felt	7
Feather (can purchase at craft store)	9
Field guide (birds)	8
Field guide (sea shells)	27
Flexible wire	24
Flour	21c
Food coloring	28
Goldfish snack crackers	11
Gummy worms	31
Hair/fur from 2 or more mammals	3
Hydras (live)	28c
Index cards	22
Liquid bluing	28
Magnifying glass	9, 24, 25

Supplies needed (see lessons for details)	Lesson
Marshmallows (large and small)	24
Microscope and slides	32
Modeling clay	13, 25, 26c
Newspaper	21c
Owl pellet (optional)	10
Pipe cleaners	22, 24, 26c
Plastic zipper bags	7
Pond water	32
Poster board/tag board	7, 29
Rubber/plastic gloves	29c
Salt	28
Sand dollar (dead and dried; check at craft store—optional)	29
Spider web (optional)	24
Starfish (dead and dried; check at craft store—optional)	29
Salt dough	29
Scarves	23
Sequins or flat beads	16
Sea shells	27
Sleeping bag	23
Soap (anti-bacterial hand)	33
Sponge (natural—optional)	30
Sponge (synthetic)	30
Starfish (preserved for dissection)	29c
Stopwatch	6
String	21c
Styrofoam balls	22
Tadpoles and tank (optional)	15
Tape (cloth)	19
Tempera paints	30
Toothbrush	6
Toothpicks	22, 24
Yarn	32

Works Cited

Adams, A. B. *Eternal Quest: The Story of the Great Naturalists.* New York: G.P. Putnam's Sons, 1969.

Bargar, Sherie, and Linda Johnson. *Rattlesnakes.* Vero Beach: Rourke Enterprises, Inc., 1986.

"Birds." http://www.earthlife.net/birds.

Cardwardine, Mark, et.al. *Whales, Dolphins & Porpoises.* Sydney: US Weldon Owen Inc., 1998.

Chinery, Michael. *Butterfly.* Mahwah: Troll Associates, 1991.

Chinery, Michael. *Shark.* Mahwah: Troll Associates, 1991.

Coldrey, Jennifer. *Shells.* New York: Dorling Kindersley, Inc., 1993.

Cole, Joanna. *A Bird's Body.* New York: William Morrow & Co., 1982.

Cousteau Society. *Corals: The Sea's Great Builders.* New York: Simon & Shuster, 1992.

'Espinasse, M. *Robert Hooke.* Berkeley: University of California, 1962.

Evans, J. Edward. *Charles Darwin Revolutionary Biologist.* Minneapolis: Lerner Publications, 1993.

Fleisher, Paul. *Gorillas.* New York: Benchmark Books, 2001.

Gish, Duane T., Ph.D. *The Amazing Story of Creation.* El Cajon: Institute for Creation Research, 1990.

"Georges Cuvier." http://www.ucmp.berkeley.edu/history/cuvier.

Gowell, Elizabeth Tayntor. *Whales and Dolphins What They Have in Common.* New York: Franklin Watts, 1999.

Ham, Ken. *The Great Dinosaur Mystery Solved!* Green Forest: Master Books, 1999.

Hird, Ed. "Dr. Louis Pasteur: Servant of All." *Deep Cove Crier.* December 1997.

Jackson, Tom. *Nature's Children Rattlesnakes.* Danbury: Grolier Educational, 2001.

Kalman, Bobbie, and Allison Larin. *What is a Fish?* New York: Crabtree Publishers, 1999.

Koerner, L. *Linnaeus: Nature and Nation.* Cambridge: Harvard University, 1999.

Lacey, Elizabeth A. *The Complete Frog a Guide for the Very Young Naturalist.* New York: Lothrop, Lee & Shepard Books, 1989.

Landau, Elaine. *Sea Horses.* New York: Children's Press, 1999.

Lindroth, S. *The Two Faces of Linnaeus.* Berkeley: University of California Press, 1983.

"Louis Pasteur." http://web.ukonline.co.uk/b.gardner/pasteur.htm.

Maynard, Thane. *Primates Apes, Monkeys, Prosimians.* New York: Franklin Watts, 1994.

Markle, Sandra. *Outside and Inside Kangaroos.* New York: Atheneum Books for Young Readers, 1999.

Moore, J. A. *Science as a Way of Knowing.* Cambridge: Harvard University Press, 1993.

Morris, John D., Ph.D. *The Young Earth.* Colorado Springs: Master Books, 1994.

National Geographic Book of Mammals. Washington, D.C.: National Geographic Society, 1998.

Parker, Gregory et al. *Biology: God's Living Creation.* Pensacola: A Beka Books, 1997.

Parker, Steve. *Charles Darwin and Evolution.* London: HarperCollins Publishers, 1992.

Ross, Michael E. *Wormology.* Minneapolis: Carolrhoda Books, Inc., 1996.

Rudwick, M.J. S. *The Meaning of Fossils.* Chicago: University of Chicago Press, 1985.

Scholastic Voyages of Discovery Mammals. New York: Scholastic, Inc., 1997.

Stone, Lynn M. *Tasmanian Devil.* Vero Beach: Rourke Corptoration, Inc., 1990.

Swan, Erin Pembrey. *Meat-eating Marsupials.* New York: Franklin Watts, 2002.

Swan, Erin Pembrey. *Primates: From Howler Monkeys to Humans.* New York: Franklin Watts, 1998.

Taylor, Leighton. *Jellyfish.* Minneapolis: Lerner Publishing Co., 1998.

VanCleave, Janice. *Biology for Every Kid.* New York: John Wiley & Sons, Inc., 1990.

VanCleave, Janice. *Insects and Spiders.* New York: John Wiley & Sons, Inc., 1998.

VanCleave, Janice. *Play and Find Out About Bugs.* New York: John Wiley & Sons, Inc., 1999.

Walters, Martin. *The Simon & Schuster Young Readers' Book of Animals.* New York: Simon & Schuster, Inc., 1990.